A
FIELD GUIDE TO
EAST LONDON
WILDLIFE

A Field Guide To East London Wildlife First Edition
Copyright © Hoxton Mini Press 2014. All rights reserved.
Images adapted from original etchings by Ian McDonnell
Layout and Design by Ian McDonnell
Text by Harry Adès

A CIP catalogue record for this book is available from the British Library. ISBN: 978-0-9576998-5-4
First published in the United Kingdom in 2014 by Hoxton Mini Press
No part of this publication may be reproduced, stored in a retrieval system, or transmitted in any form
or by any means, electronic, mechanical, photocopying, recording or otherwise, without the prior written
permission of the copyright owner.

Printed and bound by: RRD, China
This book and associated prints and products can be ordered from www.hoxtonminipress.com

A
FIELD GUIDE TO
EAST LONDON
WILDLIFE

Images: **IAN MCDONNELL**
Words: **HARRY ADÈS**

HOXTON MINI PRESS

CONTENTS

INTRODUCTION

Why does East London need a field guide? London is a green city, the greenest city of its size in the world. Yet for outsiders East London is rarely associated with open spaces and abundant wildlife.

The horrors of its Victorian past still linger. The old East End, long the repository for the rural poor, immigrants and refugees, became in the industrial age a nightmare of filthy slums and dead-end rookeries. What place had the natural world in this ultimate urban dystopia?

We live in different times. The slums were cleared more than a century ago, and the area's rich history is keenly celebrated, not reviled. Young new communities continue to come East, bringing with them a hope, ambition and energy that make this one of London's most exciting places to be.

East London is still urban, about as urban as it gets. Does that matter? The heavy imprint of our species has marked almost everything we see, whether we're in the terraces of Hackney or the fields of Hampshire. Our urban and rural landscapes are both highly managed, manmade environments, and the natural world must carve out its existence in the margins we have left for it.

What do animals really know of cities? What they know is opportunity. The habit of life is to find a niche. Within the incredible waste generated by cities, comes incredible potential for the resourceful.

It's telling how many successful urban animals are highly intelligent or highly adaptable – the magpie, squirrel, crow, pigeon and fox, for example, are ordinary creatures with extraordinary brains. How many others have been able to recast manmade objects as natural features – the herring gull's substitution of office roofs for sea cliffs, or the peregrine falcon perched on skyscrapers instead of rocky spires? Then there are those that do better in the city than in the fields, the frogs and bees who find sanctuary in concrete, away from farmers' machinery and chemicals. At the other end of the spectrum, less ecologically nimble creatures like the hedgehog are falling by the roadside.

This field guide smashes the traditional divisions between town and country, human and natural, domesticated and wild. The fox slips between pavement and pasture as necessity dictates; the deer trades dense forest for suburban forage without worrying about tarmac; domesticated doves and parakeets break free and become feral; immigrants – or if you are so minded, invaders – the carp, the grey squirrel, the terrapin, glut on ill-defended indigenes; stowaways and smuggled goods bring exotic colour to grey streets; accessories and adornments such as pocket pigs and ferrets become fireside pets. Such fusions seem to come easiest in this place of dynamic extremes, making it possible for East London to nurture its own unique menagerie.

1
PIGEON
Columba livia

The pigeon is a dove with a PR problem. Even Bill Oddie says all they are good for is food for falcons – and he loves birds. Tower Hamlets council agreed, and has employed a hawk to deter pigeons.

But pigeons have much to be proud about. They are extremely intelligent, can recognise faces and letters, and have worked out how to use the Tube to get around London.

They are also the most decorated of any animal used in war, winning 32 Dickin Medals for gallantry – exactly 32 more than Bill Oddie.

ABSOLUTE ESSENTIALS

• *feet are often deformed because toes get tangled in garbage and fall off*

• *tiny iron balls in their ears help them navigate the Earth's magnetic field*

• *do not leave nest until 2 months old, making it hard to spot baby pigeons*

2
HEDGEHOG
Erinaceus europaeus

Britain's only mammal to protect itself with spines actually isn't faring that well.

In the last decade, numbers have declined by more than a third and they are continuing to fall. In the 1950s, there were 36 million hedgehogs, but now there are fewer than a million. They are fast disappearing from London too.

Roads are a problem. They break up habitats and make isolated populations more susceptible to disease. Tens of thousands are mown down by road traffic each year. In fact, hedgehog road kill is how scientists measure hedgehog numbers: the more that are dead, the bigger the population must be.

ABSOLUTE ESSENTIALS

- *a saucer of milk will give them diarrhea; water is much better*

- *known as the 'gardener's friend' because of its appetite for slugs, snails and caterpillars*

- *born with soft spines to make it easier for mother*

3
GREY SQUIRREL
Sciurus carolinensis

Introduced from North America in 1876, the grey squirrel has been spectacularly successful in securing its place as the capital's cutest rodent – even though many people can't forgive it for elbowing out the even cuter, native red squirrel.

Faster, bigger, stronger and more adaptable than their cousins, greys are much better at processing proteins and energy from acorns and will outperform reds in such habitats, not least London parks and gardens.

Stories periodically surface of crack-addicted squirrels desperately digging up front gardens to find drug dealers' hidden stashes. Scotland Yard denies this.

ABSOLUTE ESSENTIALS

- *its crib (home) is called a drey (nest)*
- *if watched will pretend to bury food while hiding it in cheeks*
- *will die if it eats crack cocaine, according to the RSPCA*

4
MARBLED WHITE BUTTERFLY
Melanargia galathea

Like many Londoners, this distinctive butterfly has little knowledge of the far north of the country, and no desire to go there.

It prefers southern downlands, and does well in the capital by making do with grassy verges by roads and railways, drifting into gardens for an occasional flowery treat.

ABSOLUTE ESSENTIALS

- *female doesn't lay, but rather drops its egg from a perch or while flying*

- *plays host to a tiny red blood-sucking parasitic mite*

- *favours purple flowers*

5
BEES
Apis mellifera mellifera

The honey bees of St Mary's Secret Garden in Hackney have an advantage over their comrades in the countryside. The huge diversity of city-garden blooms and the longer flowering season lend a depth and complexity to their honey that their neighbours can't rival.

While bee populations are slumping across the world, London's numbers are rising – to such an extent that there's concern there won't be enough flowers to go round. Good thing for the Hackney bees that Columbia Road is just a short buzz away.

ABSOLUTE ESSENTIALS

• *males don't have a sting*

• *communicate with each other through the medium of 'dance'*

• *can discern colours, flavours and odours*

6
DOMESTIC CAT
Felis Catus

Cats were probably domesticated in Neolithic times, when humans discovered that storing grain led to a mouse problem.

The cat's primary function as rodent control officer has now shifted to furry de-stress unit. London's first cat café opened in Shoreditch in 2014, providing a form of no-strings feline pet rental – with coffee and cake.

Unfortunately, research has found that most cats don't like being stroked that much. Contrary to popular wisdom, when a cat rolls over and exposes its belly, the last thing it wants is a tummy rub.

ABSOLUTE ESSENTIALS

• *shows stress by flattening ears*

• *cannot climb head first down a tree*

• *lands on its feet by extreme twisting while conserving angular momentum*

7
CARP
Cyprinus carpio

There are some big carp grubbing along the beds of the Walthamstow reservoirs. The largest fish found there was a 45lb mirror carp, caught during an all-night session in 2011.

Carp are not native to the UK but were introduced by monks from Eastern Europe in the Middle Ages for farming in 'stew ponds'. They soon became naturalised and now flourish in most of our rivers and lakes.

ABSOLUTE ESSENTIALS

- *can live 45 years in captivity and grow to 5ft in length*
- *teeth located at the back of the throat*
- *considered the 'fox of the river' for their cunning*

CITY FARM ANIMALS

City farms in Hackney, Stepney, Newham, Spitalfields, Leyton and the Isle of Dogs provide East London communities with a flavour of the rural farmyard.

MONGREL

Canis lupus familiaris

Dog snobs won't hear a word of it, but evidence is stacking up in favour of mongrels over purebred dogs. Mongrels often score higher in intelligence tests, and may be less susceptible to health issues that arise through inbreeding.

More than 300 stray dogs are found every day in the UK, many of them mongrels. Some are cared for by society's other 'strays', homeless people.

Many say their dogs are their treasured and most loyal companions, whom they depend on for their emotional survival in difficult times. Above all, they say their dogs won't judge them as strangers so often do.

ABSOLUTE ESSENTIALS

- *Scruffts is a recent addition to the Crufts dog show, especially for mongrels*

- *the charity Dogs Trust provides free veterinary treatments for dogs of homeless owners*

- *mongrels live on average 1.8 years longer than pedigree dogs*

10
CROW
Corvus corone

It eats just about anything – insects, spiders, eggs, nestlings, seeds, vegetables, discarded food – and especially dead animals, hence its proper name, carrion crow. It will even work with other crows to harry predators for their kill.

Cautious of humans, but not afraid, they quickly learn if they have been tricked off food. The bane of farmers since the birth of agriculture, crows work together to find safe places to eat – and to exploit any weakness for a square meal.

ABSOLUTE ESSENTIALS

• *the collective noun is a 'murder' of crows*

• *one crow species has a command of causal reasoning similar to a 5-year-old child*

• *drops nuts on to roads and waits for traffic to crack them*

11
CHICKEN
Gallus gallus domesticus

Look down an East London high street and you'd think there were more chicken shops than chickens.

For every school in Tower Hamlets, there are 42 fast-food outlets, while in next-door Newham no school is more than 500m away from one. Most of them are chicken shops and more are appearing all the time.

Fried chicken is the tucker of choice, because it's quick, cheap and filling. It's also very salty and full of fat. Newham has the highest prevalence of diabetes among London boroughs.

ABSOLUTE ESSENTIALS

• *there are three chickens for every person in the world*

• *200,000 British households keep their own hens*

• *more than a third of all UK sandwiches sold are chicken*

12
EEL
Anguilla anguilla

If the East End can be indentified with a particular culinary creation, it is the jellied eel.

When boiled, eels produce a gelatinous gloop, which cools into jelly. Prepared with vinegar, nutmeg and lemon, the dish has been popular in the East End since at least the 18th century, and enjoyed a revival during the Second World War when fresh, cheap, nutritious food was hard to come by.

There are still more than a dozen eel and pie shops in the East End, but as the regulars get older or are priced out to the suburbs, fewer can afford to keep their doors open. Like the eels they dish up, the shops are becoming critically endangered species.

ABSOLUTE ESSENTIALS

• *spawns in the Sargasso Sea*

• *larvae drift for 300 days towards European rivers*

• *life cycle was unknown until 1920*

13
SWAN
Cygnus olor

Swans gather at Walthamstow reservoirs. The most common is the mute swan, so called because it's relatively quiet. But a soft voice hides a territorial temperament that swiftly becomes aggressive when threatened.

At nesting time, a loud hiss could signal they're planning to thump you with the hard bone in their wings – but it's rare. They're not thought to be strong enough to break a healthy adult's arm.

ABSOLUTE ESSENTIALS

- *unmarked swans on open water are the property of the monarch*

- *wing beats in flight can be heard a mile away*

- *threat display with wings half lifted and neck coiled back is called 'busking'*

14
CONFUSED WHALE
Whales occasionally make a wrong turn into the
Thames, including in recent years two humpbacks and
a northern bottlenose whale, none of which survived.

15
FERRET
Mustela putorius furo

The ferret is essentially a polecat with good manners. It's a domesticated version, originally used for hunting rabbits and chasing ground-dwelling rodents out of their burrows.

Their love for dark, confined spaces was exploited by Yorkshire coal miners in the sport of ferret legging. Contestants stuff live ferrets down their trousers. The winner is the one who lasts the longest.

The ferret is now less a trouser athlete than a fashion accessory paraded in the parks of East London by soft southerners, who like to keep them only as charming, cuddly, razor-toothed pets.

ABSOLUTE ESSENTIALS

- *world record for ferret legging is 5 hours 30 minutes*

- *underwear is not allowed*

- *nor is filing down the ferret's teeth*

BULL MASTIFF

Canis lupus familiaris

Often confused with the pit bull, the bull mastiff is not a fighting dog but a guard dog, originally bred by Victorian gamekeepers for use against poachers.

It's a popular status dog on the estates of East London for its strength, stamina and loyalty – so popular that illegal breeders try to cash in. Unwanted litters are often left abandoned.

Around half the dogs taken into Battersea Dogs Home each year are bull breeds, and many have been involved in dog fighting.

ABSOLUTE ESSENTIALS

• *puts on weight easily and is prone to bloat*

• *London is the second safest region in the country for dog bites*

• *dog attacks are three times more likely in deprived areas*

LOST BABY ELEPHANT
Elephas maximus

The capital hasn't had a resident elephant since 2001, when London Zoo's last three packed their trunks for more spacious quarters at Whipsnade.

Consequently, any elephants that are seen in or around Bethnal Green station are likely to be lost, at the very least.

ABSOLUTE ESSENTIALS

- *same-sex relationships common and less fleeting than heterosexual hook-ups*

- *sleeps standing up*

- *does without pelvic thrusts when mating thanks to a highly flexible penis*

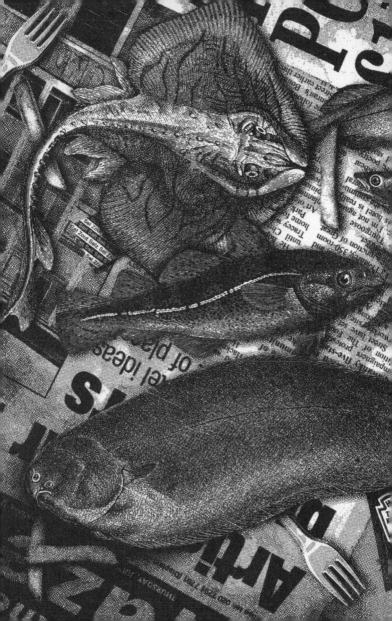

18
WHITE FISH
White fish popular on the dinner plate include cod,
haddock, hake, coley, sole, plaice, skate and pollack.

19
FOX
Vulpes vulpes

It wasn't until the 1930s that foxes established themselves in London, and now about 10,000 of them roam our streets.

A fox attack on sleeping baby twins in a house near Victoria Park in 2010 sparked fears that urban foxes were becoming too numerous and aggressive, but there's little evidence either. Numbers are stable and attacks remain extremely rare.

Foxes move readily between town and country – urban and rural foxes are essentially the same. Foxes in the city can be bolder than their country counterparts, because their environment demands it – much like Woking commuters out for a drink in Hoxton on a Friday night.

ABSOLUTE ESSENTIALS

• *rarely live for more than two years in the wild*

• *fox populations are self-regulating, depending on food availability*

• *can hear a watch ticking from 120 feet*

COCKROACHES
Blattella germanica

East London is clearly a wonderful habitat for cockroaches. Tower Hamlets and Newham have regularly been ranked by the British Pest Control Association to be among the best places in the country to see them.

In Hackney, individual restaurants in Mare Street and Kingsland Road have also recently provided a home to these resilient insects. Unfortunately, being carriers of salmonella and E. coli, the council decided to cut short their residency.

ABSOLUTE ESSENTIALS

• *UK nurtures two main species, the German and oriental*

• *the German cockroach reproduces faster than any other cockroach*

• *in Germany it is known as the Russian cockroach*

21
FROG
Rana temporaria

If you're a frog, the countryside is no longer the place to bring up the kids. Common frogs, once found everywhere, are deserting agrichemical-coated farming land for urban gardens and city sewers.

Installing a garden water feature is shrewd horticultural strategy. Even modest ponds can become the birthing pools for hordes of frogs that like nothing more than dining out on plant-destroying slugs and snails.

ABSOLUTE ESSENTIALS

• *females lay up to 2,000 eggs at a time*

• *call is a low rasp, not a 'ribbit'*

• *can adjust skin tone to blend in with surroundings*

22
RETIRED GREYHOUND
Canis lupus familiaris

Greyhound track racing using an artificial lure was invented in 1876 in London. By the 1940s, the country had more than 70 tracks, with London alone enjoying 33 of them.

Nowadays, going to the dogs has itself gone to the dogs. The mighty Walthamstow stadium closed its Grade II-listed doors for good in 2008, and East London is now served by only one surviving track in Romford.

Most greyhounds are retired from racing by their fourth birthday, and specialist charities do their best to find them new homes. The racing industry says around 1,000 are put down each year, but campaigners say the true figure is much higher.

ABSOLUTE ESSENTIALS

- *unusually high levels of red blood cells and fast-twitch muscle*

- *8,000 greyhound track veterans are retired each year*

- *Born Slippy, the hit by Underworld, was a Romford greyhound the band won money on*

23
DOUBLE YELLOW LIONS
Panthera leo

Once confined to sub-Saharan African and south-west Asia, the lion is now a familiar sight in urban areas – but is a particular menace along the thoroughfares of East London.

Between them, two endemic lion species are responsible for more traffic-related inconvenience than all other animals combined.

The single yellow is highly unpredictable but generally should not be approached during daytime on weekdays or until 1.30pm on Saturdays. Double yellow lions should be avoided at all times.

ABSOLUTE ESSENTIALS

• *responsible for 775,000 traffic penalties in East London every year*

• *5,400 cars impounded for their own safety in Newham alone every year*

• *invasive species, linked to falling numbers of cars in London*

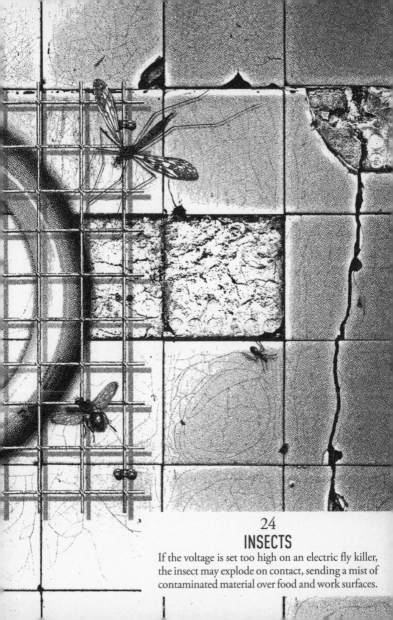

24
INSECTS
If the voltage is set too high on an electric fly killer, the insect may explode on contact, sending a mist of contaminated material over food and work surfaces.

25
WASP
Vespula vulgaris

As if they had evolved with only one purpose, wasps seem to know exactly when and where you're having your next picnic.

In fact, it's only an issue in mid-to-late summer, after the queen stops laying eggs and there are fewer hungry grubs in the nest. Up till then, worker wasps feed the grubs and are rewarded with secretions of sugary goo. When those treats stop coming, the workers go out on the hunt for anything sweet.

They love fermenting fruit even more than the dregs of your pint, and it makes them just as tipsy – and aggressive.

ABSOLUTE ESSENTIALS

- *voracious predators of garden pests and insects*

- *build nests from paper – mashed up pieces of wood fibre and plant stems*

- *unlike bees, wasps do not swarm*

26
HERRING GULL
Larus argentatus

Ask Eric Cantona this: when the trawlers stop throwing sardines into the sea, where do the seagulls go?

Many have gone to London, where the ready supply of discarded food, bin bags and rubbish dumps provides a smorgasbord for several species of gull, including the herring gull, known for its boisterous and sometimes destructive behaviour.

Swapping cliffs for office blocks and tall buildings, gulls can nest on rooftops safely out of the reach of predators. The formula is so good that many seem to be breaking their connection with the sea all together.

ABSOLUTE ESSENTIALS

- *'seagull' is not a species, just a descriptive word*
- *may dive-bomb anyone who gets too close to its fledglings during nesting season*
- *can drink sea water and excrete salt through its nostrils*

HORSE

Equus ferus caballus

Hackney has a centuries-old connection with horses. When just a small village outside London, horses were reared and grazed on its open pastures. The name 'hackney' itself became associated with a type of riding or 'ambling' horse, which was used for hire and later gave rise to the 'hackney carriage' – a term still used for taxis.

Nowadays, the horses you're most likely to see around Hackney are there to control crowds. A single mounted officer is considered to be as effective as twelve on the ground.

ABSOLUTE ESSENTIALS

• *there are nine police stables in London*

• *police horses wear rubber studs for grip on tarmac and stealth*

• *jaca in Spanish and haquenée in French are related to 'hackney', and refer to a type of horse*

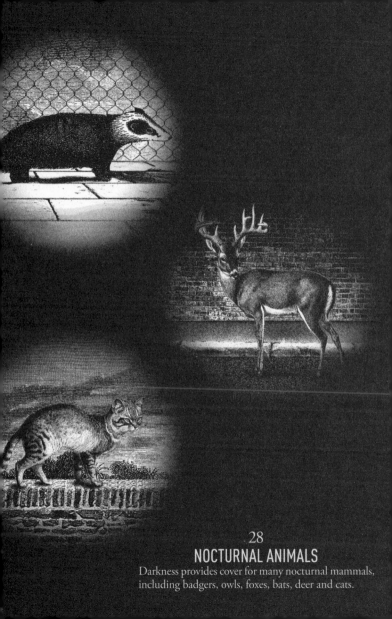

NOCTURNAL ANIMALS
Darkness provides cover for many nocturnal mammals,
including badgers, owls, foxes, bats, deer and cats.

29

HOUSE SPARROW
Passer domesticus

East Londoners might be proud about being called 'cockney sparrows', a term that seems to match their chirpy, quick-witted banter and resilience.

They might be less happy to know that their namesake birds are sex-crazed psychopaths, comparatively speaking. Prone to bigamy, incest and infanticide, the house sparrow has a reputation for lechery, with frequent copulation and repeated mounting between pairs.

ABSOLUTE ESSENTIALS

- *eggs have been considered aphrodisiacs since antiquity*
- *world's most widely distributed wild bird*
- *rare now in central London and in steep decline across the UK*

30

KESTREL
Falco tinnunculus

Kestrels are expert vole hunters. With special ultraviolet vision, they can see the trails of urine that voles leave as they wander about, making them easy prey.

In East London, where voles are in short supply, they make do with sparrows and other small birds.

Facing the breeze, they can hover perfectly for long periods by matching the wind speed by rapidly beating their wings. They were once known as 'windfuckers' or 'fuckwinds', in the old sense of fuck meaning to beat.

ABSOLUTE ESSENTIALS

- *weighs about the same as a vinyl record*
- *400 nesting pairs in London*
- *lowest-ranking bird of prey in medieval falconry*

31
MALLARD
Anas platyrhynchos

Feeding bread to the ducks in Victoria Park is for many toddlers their first close interaction with wild animals. For some it will be the beginning of a lifelong love of birds.

It's ironic that this practice is now considered harmful.

Bread is junk food for mallards. It fills them with nutrient-light carbohydrate, when they can fend for themselves perfectly well in any season. Grain, oats, rice, birdseed and vegetable trimmings are much healthier alternatives.

ABSOLUTE ESSENTIALS

• *mouldy bread is even worse*

• *only females make the classic 'quack' sound*

• *penis is corkscrew shaped, but vagina is a reverse corkscrew which relaxes only for favoured mate*

32

FERAL CATS
Felis catus

If it had the inclination, an unspayed female cat could have 420,000 offspring in just seven years.

Economic hardship has led to an unprecedented numbers of stray and abandoned cats on London's streets. Feral cat colonies favour wasteland and industrial estates, such as the Ford plant at Dagenham, where they are little disturbed.

It's not known how many cats are abandoned each year, but the more than 50 cat rescue and re-homing centres based around the capital are some indication.

ABSOLUTE ESSENTIALS

- *the charity Cats Protection neuters a cat at least every three minutes*

- *kittens sleep 18 hours a day; their growth hormones are only released during sleep*

- *cats can become pregnant from four months old*

33
SMUGGLED ANIMALS
Illegal trade in endangered or controlled species, including giant
African snails, eaten as a delicacy, and snakes and pangolins,
used in Chinese medicine, continues to be a problem.

34

DONKEY
Equus asinus

The traditional role of donkey as beast of burden is largely obsolete in our automated and mechanised city.

They are beasts of levity now, bringing good cheer rather than heavy loads.

From donkey rides at Spitalfields City Farm to the annual donkey derby at Theydon Bois, they give delight to children – while maintaining a steady air of utter dejection.

ABSOLUTE ESSENTIALS

- *donkeys used to be sold by Irish Travellers at a dedicated market in Islington*

- *donkey is a relatively new word for 'ass', first appearing only in the 1780s*

- *unlike ass, the word 'donkey' is rarely taken to mean 'bottom'*

35
MAGPIE
Pica pica

Since medieval times the magpie has been associated with bad luck. The famous rhyme 'One for sorrow' has many variations, but encountering a lone magpie is unwaveringly bad.

Magpies mate in the same pair for life; therefore, if one is seen alone, it's an ill omen. Saluting the lone magpie and asking after its family supposes all is well with it – and is considered a way of warding off evil.

Superstitious people are now doffing their hats to magpies more than ever – magpie numbers have quadrupled in the last 40 years.

ABSOLUTE ESSENTIALS

- *highly intelligent*
- *won't travel far from the place it was hatched*
- *thought to hoard shiny objects to attract a mate*

36

PARTY ANIMAL
Homo jubilensis

The antics of this gregarious nocturnal primate, typically found around Hoxton Square and Shoreditch High Street, tend to become tiresome in the small hours, as good-natured high-spirits develop into increasingly functionless behaviour.

At the climax of night-time forays, unruly packs compete with each other in exchanges of shouting and tuneless singing that sometimes turn aggressive.

When threatened, individuals may shoot out hot arcs of vomit and urine, before collapsing and playing dead in the gutter.

ABSOLUTE ESSENTIALS

* *listless, unsteady gait*
* *enjoys shameless exhibitionism among peers*
* *occasionally seen after dawn in a confused state*

37

RAT

Rattus norvegicus

According to some newspapers, 'mutant super rats' the size of small cats are stalking the streets of London, immune to conventional poisons, and scaring the bejesus out of pest controllers.

In Ridley Road Market, the fightback has already begun. Several butchers there were caught selling rat meat – though it wasn't sewer rats, but the more flavoursome cane rat variety from Ghana.

ABSOLUTE ESSENTIALS

- *emit ultrasonic chirps when happy*
- *it's a myth you're never more than 6ft away from a rat in London*
- *current estimates put the true figure at 164ft*

38

ROSE-RINGED PARAKEET
Psittacula krameri

Lending a flash of tropical colour to London skies, and the sounds of the jungle to Waltham Forest, the rose-ringed parakeet looks far from home.

Originating from the Indian subcontinent, they have been popular pets since the 19th century, but only started breeding in the wild near London in 1969. Some say that Jimi Hendrix released a couple in Carnaby Street to bring exotic psychedelia to the city.

There are now thought to be well over 30,000 of them in and around the capital, but their effect on native species isn't well understood. The RSPB has reminded those in favour of a cull that all wild birds are protected by law, including non-native parakeets.

ABSOLUTE ESSENTIALS

- *roosts in flocks of up to 15,000 birds*
- *native to the Himalayan foothills, so can easily handle English winters*
- *can mimic the human voice*

39
MOTHS

Moths are in serious decline because of habitat loss, pollution and street lighting. Bats have learnt to hunt moths that are drawn to street lights.

40
TERRAPIN
Trachemys scripta elegans

Buy a dog, you know it's for life. Buy a baby terrapin the size of a bottle top, would you know it's a commitment of 40 years, and that it grows to the size of a dinner plate?

Now that the craze for Teenage Mutant Ninja Turtles has long passed, pet terrapins get abandoned – and wreak carnage on British waterways, gorging on native frogs, newts, dragonflies, fish, even ducklings.

It's thought to be too cold for terrapins to breed in the wild. But conservationists fear that a baby terrapin found on the Regent's Canal could have benefited from London's warmer microhabitats.

ABSOLUTE ESSENTIALS

• *native to North America*

• *one of the world's 100 most invasive species*

• *the Teenage Mutant Ninja Turtles were revealed to be terrapins. Mutant ninja terrapins.*

41
PIG
Sus scrofa domesticus

Pigs are well-behaved, affectionate, intelligent, and they never willingly soil their living quarters. They would surely have been household pets long ago, but for a very large detail: they can grow to be 6ft long and weigh 350kg.

Enter the miniature pig – also known as a micro, pocket, mini or teacup pig – bred to be small and manageable. Originally used for medical research, scientists discovered a new principle – that cuteness is inversely proportional to size.

They're so cute that even Shoreditch hipsters are proud to trot the pavements at their side. Pig walkers do need a special licence, and register as a smallholder. And if they get bored of them, there's always bacon.

ABSOLUTE ESSENTIALS

• *shouldn't top 18 inches in height*

• *costs up to £700 to buy*

• *no guarantee that a micro pig will stay small*

42
MICE
Mus musculus

For Hackney hipsters, mice are so much more than house pests that nibble the cornflakes packet and leave dozens of little black 'calling cards' everywhere. Nor are they merely the potential vectors of diseases as exciting as rickettsialpox, leptospirosis and bubonic plague.

They are the focus of a craze for 'anthropomorphic taxidermy' – gutting, stuffing, dressing, and arranging your dead rodent into human poses and tableaux. Best of all, the world HQ for this craft is conveniently located for hipsters on Mare Street.

ABSOLUTE ESSENTIALS

• *eat their own faeces*

• *do not vomit*

• *after mating, females develop a 'copulation plug' to prevent further advances*